History's Witches

An illustrated guide

Written & Illustrated by Lisa Graves

This book is dedicated to the most
talented artists I know- Finn & Stella.

ISBN: 9781623955168 • eISBN: 9781623955175
ePib ISBN: 9781623955182
Published in the United States
by Xist Publishing
www.xistpublishing.com

A History of Witches

Throughout time, various women (and some men) were accused of being witches. Many, if not all were persecuted in different ways, and had their lives turned upside-down. They lost their homes, their property, their families, and more. A "witch" was a very broad term for a woman who was thought to have evil or magical powers.

A woman was accused of witchcraft for many reasons:

POLITICAL

Certain women, such as Anne Boleyn or Catherine de Medici, held very powerful positions in court. Many people around them sought to steal this power in order to advance their own political agendas.

RELIGIOUS

Women like Jeanne Guyon were labeled witches for simply disagreeing or disobeying the church.

MENTAL ILLNESS

Some of these women suffered from undiagnosed mental illness, and because these afflictions were so unfamiliar to the people around them, they were convicted as witches.

GREED

Certain folks would point at their neighbor yelling, "witch," just because they wanted to aquire more land.

MIDWIVES

Many many midwives/healers were persecuted for witchcraft while trying to help the sick. When their cures and healing treatments did not work, the family wanted to blame someone for their loss.

This book is an illustrated tribute to thirteen different women who were falsely accused of witchcraft. Their stories could be compared to today's bullying. Each was pushed around by parents, an army, a father-in-law, a step-son, the church, a king, a patient, a kingdom, an acquaintance, greedy neighbors, or a bishop.

Eleanor of Aquitaine

ELEANOR OF AQUITAINE (1122-1204)
One of the richest and most powerful women during the Middle Ages, Eleanor was married to Louis VII and and became Queen of France. After his death, she married Henry II and was crowned Queen of England. She was a well-known supporter of the arts and was well educated in diplomacy, art, history, and languages. As an outspoken and feared queen, Eleanor was never persecuted as a witch, but rumors circulated when she accompanied her troops on a crusade to Jerusalem, when her husband's mistress was found dead, and when her sons revolted against her husband.

POWERFUL EDUCATED

WEALTHY LEGENDARY

RESPECTED IMPORTANT

REVERED BELOVED

REGAL FRENCH

FASHIONABLE RUTHLESS

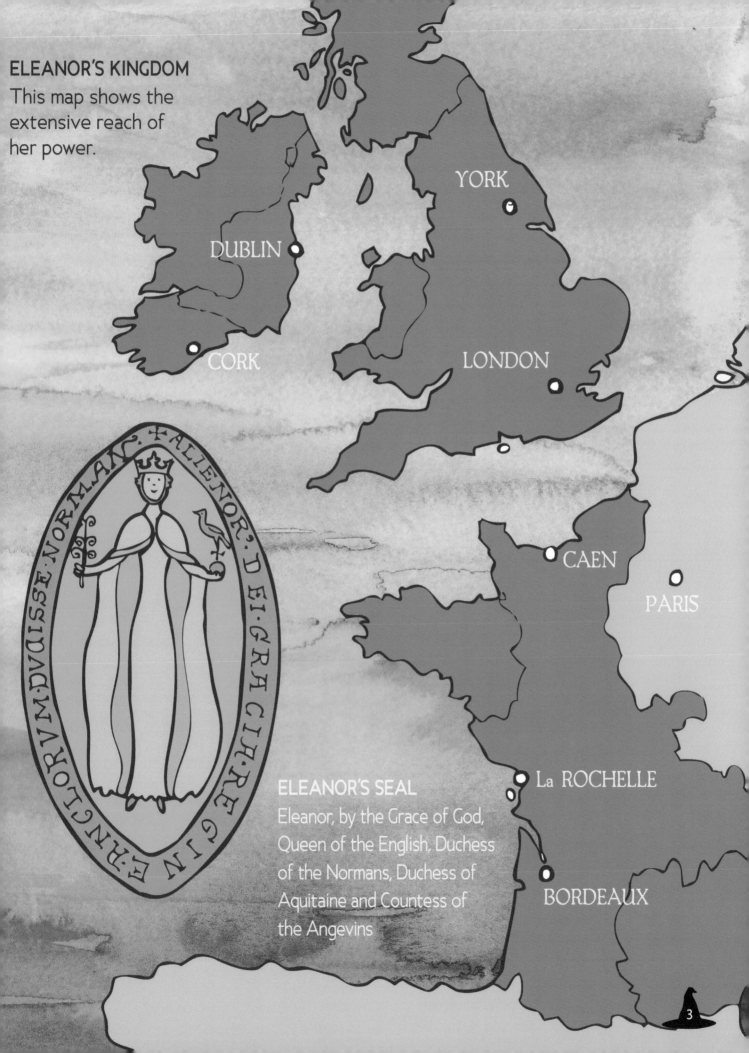

ELEANOR'S KINGDOM
This map shows the extensive reach of her power.

YORK

DUBLIN

CORK

LONDON

CAEN

PARIS

ELEANOR'S SEAL
Eleanor, by the Grace of God, Queen of the English, Duchess of the Normans, Duchess of Aquitaine and Countess of the Angevins

La ROCHELLE

BORDEAUX

3

SAINT CATHERINE OF SIENA (1347-1380) is one of two patron Saints of Italy (the other is St. Francis of Assisi). Her mother had 25 children, but more than half of them had already died when Catherine was born.

After having visions of Jesus, she took an oath of chastity (a vow not to marry, but to dedicate her life to God). When Catherine's older sister died, her mother wanted Catherine to marry a local widower. In protest, she cut her long hair and started to pray and fast (a decision to abstain from food). Her parents decided to let her serve others instead of marry.

She was able to take care of sick people, write letters to important political and religious leaders about her visions, and feed the poor, but she still continued to refuse food.

Her extreme devotion to God caused some speculation and rumors. During this time there was a fine line between divine visions and witchcraft. Some believed that the only way one could not eat for such long periods of time involved pacts with the devil.

Her level of devotion paired with the stigmata, visions, and work for the church was why she was canonized as a Saint in 1461.

COAT OF ARMS
Given to her by Charles VII in 1429.

"One life is all we have and we live it as we believe in living it. But to sacrifice what you are and to live without belief, that is a fate more terrible than dying."

Beaurevoir
Compieane
Rouen
Reims
Paris
Vaucouleurs
Orleans
Domremy
Chinon

FRANCE

Joan of Arc

A map of her journey through France.

JOAN OF ARC (1412-1431)

An illiterate peasant girl from Eastern France, Joan led the French Army to many important victories during the 100 Years' War. She claimed to have had divine guidance, and was burned at the stake for heresy and witchcraft at the age of nineteen. These ridiculous accusations were politically motivated and were eventually overturned after her death.

POWERFUL

ILLITERATE

FOCUSED

DRIVEN

UNWAVERING

DETERMINED

YOUNG

INSPIRED

RELIGIOUS

Agnes Bernauer

AGNES BERNAUER (1410-1435) Agnes was a commoner who fell in love with a Duke, Albert III of Bavaria. His father didn't approve of their relationship so he had Agnes condemned for witchcraft and drowned in the Danube River.

GERMAN

SWEET

INNOCENT

BEAUTIFUL

A COMMONER

CONFIDENT

LOVED

REMEMBERED

CELEBRATED

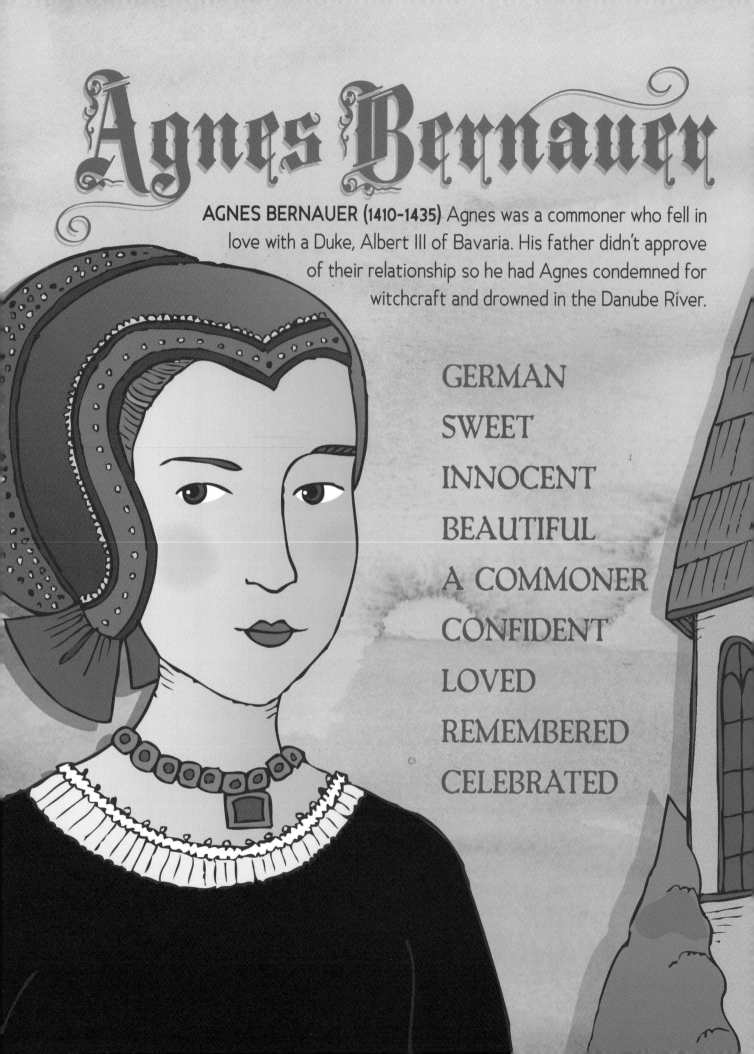

THE AGNES BERNAUER ROSE
A light pink rose named for this lovely girl.

AGNES BERNAUER CHAPEL
One of three chapels in the cemetery of the Church of Saint Peter in Straubing, Germany.

To this day, Agnes' story has been depicted in many literary works and there is still a memorial mass at the chapel, once a year, in her honor.

9

Joan of Navarre

QUEEN OF ENGLAND

JEANNE DE NAVARRE (1370-1437)
was the daughter of a King, Charles II
of Navarre, and his wife Joan of Valois.

MOTHER

QUEEN

OBEDIENT

RESILIENT

LOYAL

FRENCH

UNPOPULAR

WIDOWED

QUIET

John V, Duke of Brittany

Joan's first husband died in 1399 when she was still young. They had nine children together:

- Joan of Brittany (1387-1388)
- An unnamed baby girl (1388)
- John VI, Duke of Brittany (1389-1442)
- Marie of Brittany (1391-1446)
- Margaret of Brittany (1392-1428)
- Arthur III, Duke of Brittany (1393-1458)
- Gilles of Brittany (1394-1412)
- Richard of Brittany (1395-1438)
- Blanche of Brittany (1397-1419)

King Henry IV

In 1403, Joan became Henry IV's second wife. They did not have children, but his children from his previous marraige loved her. Unfortunately, "Prince Hal" who later became King Henry V, turned on her later in life and accused her of trying to poison him.

She was convicted of witchcraft in 1419 and kept in Pevensey Castle prison for four years. She spent the rest of her days at Nottingham Castle.

Anne Boleyn

ANNE BOLEYN (1501-1536) was born into privilege, and for political reasons, she was intentionally placed in view of King Henry VIII to lure him away from his first wife, Catherine of Aragon. Anne Boleyn was well educated and manipulative, but swore loyalty to the king even as she was being executed. Henry had her tried for witchcraft when evil political forces convinced him she was an adultress.

Anne was Henry VIII's second wife. He declared himself head of the church so that he could divorce his first wife, who was unable to give birth to a son. This was very important to a king. Although Anne too, was unable to give birth to a healthy son, she had one very important daughter, Elizabeth, who grew up to be one of the most powerful women in history, Queen Elizabeth I.

ENGLISH
STUNNING
REGAL
INTELLIGENT
CLEVER
EDUCATED
TALENTED
MANIPULATIVE
LOYAL
QUEEN

The wives of Henry VIII:

Catherine of Aragon

Anne Boleyn

Jane Seymour

Anne of Cleves

Kathryn Howard

Catherine Parr

ST. EDWARD'S CROWN
Anne was the only Queen Consort to be coronated in this crown- Henry did this to prove his commitment to his new wife.

13

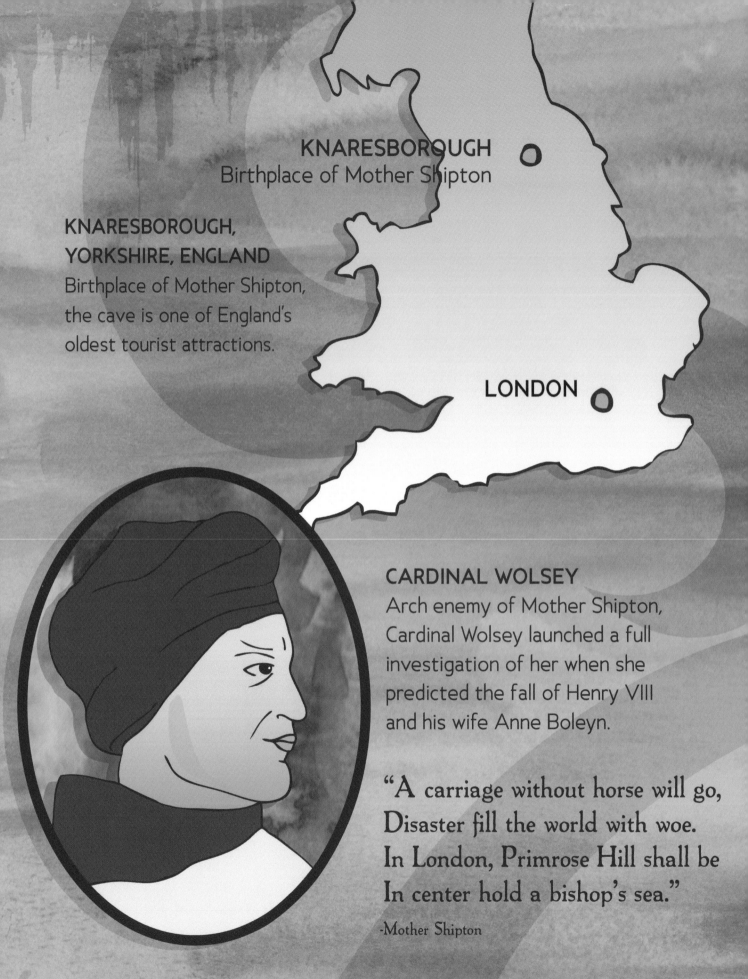

KNARESBOROUGH
Birthplace of Mother Shipton

KNARESBOROUGH, YORKSHIRE, ENGLAND
Birthplace of Mother Shipton, the cave is one of England's oldest tourist attractions.

LONDON

CARDINAL WOLSEY
Arch enemy of Mother Shipton, Cardinal Wolsey launched a full investigation of her when she predicted the fall of Henry VIII and his wife Anne Boleyn.

"A carriage without horse will go,
Disaster fill the world with woe.
In London, Primrose Hill shall be
In center hold a bishop's sea."
-Mother Shipton

Mother Shipton

URSULA SOUTHEIL (1488-1561)

Mother Shipton was born in a cave. Her mother, Agatha, had been driven out of the village she lived in by rumors and accusations. Agatha died giving birth to a deformed baby girl. As Ursula grew up, some of the villagers called her "the devil's child," but she eventually married and was considered to be very wise. Her deformities and bizarre prophecies are what led the the people of England to label her a witch.

FEARED

FEARLESS

MISUNDERSTOOD

PHYSICALLY DEFORMED

MYSTERIOUS

INTUITIVE

PROPHETIC

ORPHAN

MAGICAL

FAMILIARS

Witch hunters looked for many "signs" that a woman was, in fact, a witch. One of these signs was the presence of "familiars" or magical animals that would serve a witch and do her bidding. Ursula was accused of having four familiars who made her town sick. Her animals were a black cat named Jacke, a gray cat named Tyffen, a white lamb named Tyttey, and a black toad named Pygine.

HEALER

MIDWIFE

OUTSPOKEN

STRONG

BOLD

DEFIANT

MISUNDERSTOOD

HELPFUL

SCOURING SAND

Ursula sold her neighbor, Alice Letherdale, a bottle of homemade cleaner, but Alice refused to pay for the concoction saying she would not give money to someone who had bewitched her daughter to death.

SCOURING SAND

URSULA KEMP

Ursula was a healer and midwife born in St. Osyth, England (1525-1582).

She was often called to heal various ailments with her herbal remedies and to help women give birth. When one of her neighbors lost her child to an illness, she accused Ursula of causing the baby's death. Ursula was tried, convicted and hanged for bringing sickness to her neighbors.

Catherine de Medici

CATHERINE de' MEDICI (1519-1589) was born into the most powerful family and became the Queen Consort of France from 1547 to 1559. She was married to King Henry II, with whom she had ten children. Many of her children went on to be kings and queens all over Europe.

CHÂTEAU DE CHENONCEAU

The Château de Chenonceau is a French château located near the village of Chenonceaux, in the Loire Valley, France. It is said to have been Catherine's favorite residence. She threw lavish parties and set off the first French fireworks in the garden.

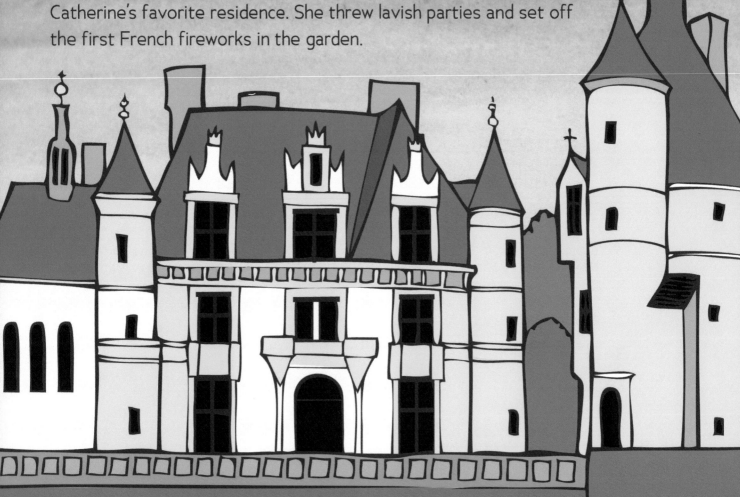

Catherine was quite a force to be reckoned with. There was nothing more important to her than making sure that her sons became kings. She was accused of witchcraft by her stepson when he thought she gave his mistress poisoned gloves. She studied the occult extensively and believed the writings of Nostradamus, a famous seer who published books of prophecies. This led many to believe she used unorthodox or even evil methods to ensure her sons' prestigious positions of power.

DECISIVE
POWERFUL
CONTROLLING
REGAL
MOTHER
QUEEN CONSORT
UNWAVERING
DEVOTED

POOR
DISABLED
DISFIGURED
MENTALLY ILL
BEGGAR
MOTHER
GRANDMOTHER
BLIND
ANGRY

Olde Mother Demdike
and the Pendle Witches

ELIZABETH SOUTHERNS (? -1612) was a very poor beggar in Lancashire, England. She was disfigured, almost blind, and most likely suffered from mental illness. She spent her days begging for food from the townspeople. When they grew tired of her groveling, they began to turn her away and deny any donations. When she mumbled under her breath while walking away, they claimed she had cursed them and their families.

She was tried as a witch with nine other women, imprisoned in Lancashire Castle, and hanged.

THE PENDLE WITCH TRIAL

One of the most famous witch trials of all time- chaos erupted between classes and families. All in all, ten women and girls were executed for witchcraft with little or no evidence but that of a disturbed child and a travelling salesman. Nowadays, Pendle is a popular tourist attraction, especially around Halloween.

Sidonia von Borcke

SIDONIA VON BORCKE (1548-1620)

Born into privilege in Stettin, Pomerania
now Szczecin, Poland. Sidonia spent mos
of her life in an abbey, a convent for
unmarried noblewomen.

CONTROVERSIAL

OUTSPOKEN

ARGUMENTATIVE

DUCHESS

POWERFUL

PRIVILEGED

OPINIONATED

CONTROLLING

INFLUENTIAL

STETTIN

Home and final resting place of Sidonia, it is now called Szczecin. It is said that the controversies surrounding her family caused the ultimate collapse of the Pomeranian Nation.

Sidonia was known for getting her nose into trouble; she filed lawsuits against family members and argued with other women at the abbey on a regular basis. One of these incidents caused the arrest of Sidonia and another resident, Dorothea von Stettin. Dorothea accused Sidonia of witchcraft in retaliation for the public humiliation of being arrested. In her trial, Sidonia was accused of the murders of her nephew, a priest, a duke, a prioress, and a gatekeeper- as well as many other crimes. All of these deaths were most likely of natural causes, but the court found her guilty and sentenced her to death.

SALEM, MASSACHUSETTS 1692

In the 17th century, Salem was inhabited by Puritans who had escaped the strict rules of England in order to practice their own religious beliefs. As land disputes arose, so did false accusations of witchcraft. Paranoia ensued and over 150 people were imprisoned. Twenty of those died by hanging or while in jail. A memorial was built in 1992 to honor those victims.

AN ACCOUNT OF THE

TRYALS

OF

Witches

NEW-ENGLAND

And the feveral remarkable Curiosities therein Occurring

"I am innocent to a Witch. I know not what a Witch is."

- Bridget Bishop, Guilty of Witchcraft

Bridget Bishop (1632-1692) was not the first person to be accused of witchcraft in Salem, MA, but she was the first to go on trial, be convicted, and then executed. She was hung on Gallows Hill on June 10, 1692.

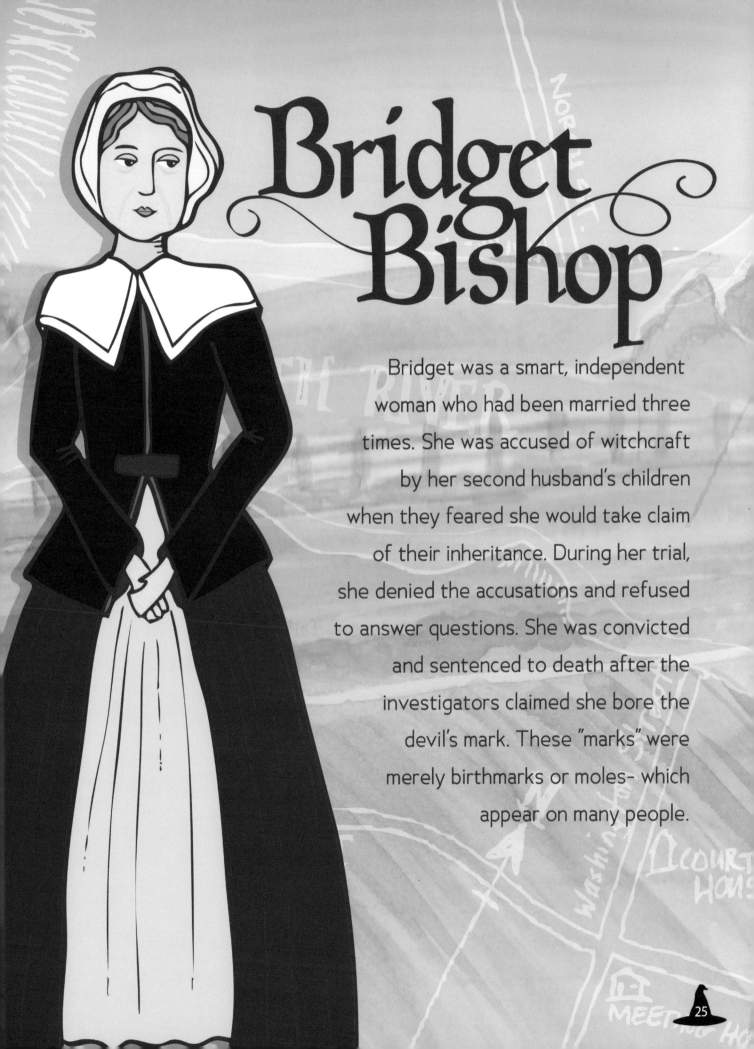

Bridget Bishop

Bridget was a smart, independent woman who had been married three times. She was accused of witchcraft by her second husband's children when they feared she would take claim of their inheritance. During her trial, she denied the accusations and refused to answer questions. She was convicted and sentenced to death after the investigators claimed she bore the devil's mark. These "marks" were merely birthmarks or moles- which appear on many people.

THE BASTILLE

Jeanne published a book called "The Short and Easy Method of Prayer." The leaders of the Roman Catholic Church in France believed that she was a member of the heretical Quietist movement. Quietism was the philosophy that it was better to be completely quiet than to pray out loud, sing hymns, or read scripture. As punishment for her beliefs, Jeanne was sent to the Bastille for four years. The Bastille was a very dangerous, very dreary prison in Paris. When Jeanne was released, she did not write any more theological books.

Jeanne Guyon

QUIET

FRENCH

SOLITARY

GENUINE

EARNEST

DEVOTED

SERIOUS

RESERVED

SPIRITUAL

WRITER

JEANNE-MARIE BOUVIER DE LA MOTTE-GUYON (1648-1717) was declared a witch by the Catholic Church for her association to members of the Quietist movement and her writings about praying constantly. She wrote that this level of devotion brought her closer to God.

For more information about the people mentioned in this book, please visit your local library. Here are some suggestions for continued reading:

The Salem Witch Trials: An Unsolved Mystery from History
by Jane Yolen and Heidi Stemple

Witches!
by Rosalyn Schanzer

Tudors and Stuarts
by Fiona Patchett

The Salem Witch Trials: An Unsolved Mystery from History
by Jane Yolen and Heidi Stemple

RECOMMENDED LINKS:
http://historywitch.com
http://thehistorychicks.com
http://tudortutor.com
http://www.elizabethan-era.org.uk

CPSIA information can be obtained
at www.ICGtesting.com
Printed in the USA
LVIC06n1604311013
359479LV00035B/336